Into The Storm
Stewarding Your Pain

Patty Nun

Into The Storm
Copyright © 2021 by Patty Nun
Published by Clay Bridges in Houston, TX
www.ClayBridgesPress.com
Cover design by Cody Johnson
Cover Photo by JackVandenHeuvel via iStockphoto

All rights reserved. No part of this publication may be reproduced, stored in a retrieval system, or transmitted in any form by any means, electronic, mechanical, photocopy, recording, or otherwise, without the prior permission of the publisher, except as provided for by USA copyright law.

ISBN: 978-1-68488-004-1
eISBN: 978-1-68488-005-8

*In loving memory of
Jordan David Nun
October 16, 1986–March 15, 2020*

Table of Contents

Foreword | vii
Endorsement | ix

Introduction | 1
The Club Nobody Wants to belong to | 3
Lament | 10
Learning to Live Without My Son | 16
Sunday Will Never Be the Same | 19
I've Got This | 22
Riding the Waves | 25
Two Pillars | 28
Coming Back | 31
On the Eve of the First Anniversary Of my Son's Death | 34
Recovery—The Twelfth Step | 37
A Semicolon and a Green Ribbon | 40
Stewarding my Pain | 45
Into the Storm | 49

Resources | 00

Foreword

It was early afternoon Sunday, March 15th, 2020. A normal Sunday routine until my cell phone rang. The voice on the phone was a close friend. In a calm voice, he said, "I need you to go take care of Patty right away, I just told her that her son has taken his own life. She is babysitting his kids at our house. Can you go right over?" My world stopped. The young man who was gone was a friend, we had been one of his customers, he was my daughter's age. Time slowed down and I rushed in slow motion to Patty. Neighbors had also been called and were there. Patty was upstairs in shock, the grandkids were preschool age, playing with their toys as the neighbors watched. I offered to watch the kids so someone could be with Patty upstairs. The three of us were aware that our friends were in the worst minutes of their lives.

Over the months since then, Patty journaled her aching heart into words. She began to share the writings with me. I felt I was reading the most sacred words one could imagine. I told her so. After several of the writings were shared, I couldn't resist asking her to consider publishing what she had written. Words fail to explain what I received reading her laments. I trust you will want to read through to the end. An ancient proverb says, "A good person can fall seven times but still stand back up." Patty has been through a season of suffering that literally took her breath away, and at least one good thing came from it, you are holding it in your hands.

Brad Brestel
Pastor and Friend

Endorsement

Everyone has pain and challenges in life - not everyone has the kind of pain Patty Nun experienced. Losing a child is the most psychological traumatic event in life, but losing them to suicide can be excruciating. How do you handle that kind of gut-wrenching pain? Patty describes how with profound wisdom and grace learned by being a mother to six, and a mental health counselor for over thirty years. She describes the loss of a child to suicide as being in a club no one wants to belong to—a club only those who have lost sons or daughters could understand. She writes as only a mother with a broken heart can and if you or someone you love has lost a child to trauma I believe you will connect to her words. Words to comfort because as Patty writes, 'Sometimes one day at a time is too hard and one step is too far, but one breath or one tear is doable.' You can survive the traumatic loss of a child and this book can show you how.

Dwight Bain
Nationally Certified Counselor
Executive Coach
Change Author

Introduction

I didn't start out writing a book. I merely was entering my thoughts in journal entries on my computer to help me make sense of what was in my head and heart by releasing my feelings and thoughts. Many times as I typed, tears ran down my face as the deepest and most difficult emotions came forth and onto the screen. I was honest with myself and wrote without resistance. Unfiltered writing allowed me to validate my emotions, to experience my thoughts. Writing has been my gateway to healing. It has been said, "If you can't feel it, you can't heal it." Each chapter is a journal entry coming out of a specific place in my journey.

Journaling is a type of self-talk. We are all involved in self-talk and the things we say to ourselves matter. While I was grieving the most painful experience of my life, the death of my thirty-three-year-old son by suicide, a second voice showed up. I am also a licensed mental health counselor and I have assisted people in the grief process. I found the professional counseling voice was trying to pull the mother out of a downward spiral into the search for a better tomorrow. The rational voice of the counselor is saying to the mother; you will have a purpose from this grief that will allow you to help others. Right now, though, you just need to be a mama and grieve and miss your boy. I reread my entries when putting them into book form and I could track how I was gradually healing from my loss. I was encouraged.

Throughout this grieving process, scriptures have sustained me. I have studied from the New American Standard Bible for over forty-three years and have memorized verses, both in the NASB as well as other versions of the Bible. Sometimes a verse came from within me as I entered my thoughts and either argued back to God or found comfort in His Word—and told Him so. I have put quotation marks around scriptural references but they may not be from a precise translation of the Bible.

Dear Reader, I don't believe you have picked up this book by accident. And, I don't know where you are in life. I do want you to know, though, whatever losses you have encountered and grief you have felt, I am so sorry for your loss. If you read something helpful to you in the following pages or can identify with something I have written that will help you process your emotions, I hope you can experience inner healing and peace.

Sometimes, one day at a time is too hard. And one step at a time is too far. But, one breath, and one tear at a time, is doable.

Patty Nun

The Club Nobody Wants to Belong to

I wasn't invited to this exclusive club, but at the moment of my son's death, I automatically became a lifetime member. My membership card is my son's Death Certificate. I guess we are called Lifers. Membership does not have age requirements, nor does it discriminate. Its membership is worldwide. Nobody judges its members. Nobody dares. Society silently acknowledges the club's existence with a deeply held respect for the unimaginable grief its members are experiencing. Once you become a member of The Club Nobody Wants to Belong to, you find yourself bonding with folks you never would have met before. We become friends. Best friends. "I'm so sorry for the loss of your child. I am sorry you had to bury your baby. My heart breaks for you. I am shattered." And it is comforting. When we meet a member, we reach out a hand. A hug. A kiss on the cheek as tears stream down our face and drop on our shoulders. Tears. Long sobs. Wailing.

Usually, tears come at the most inconvenient time. Like the powerful uncontrollable rush of a tsunami flooding everything in its way taking away my breath. Let the tears come. I remind myself, "Just take the next breath." Then as fast as the tsunami came in, it goes back to wherever it came from.

As I process through the many phases of grief over months or even years, I will eventually reach a place of "carrying this message to others," as in a Twelve-Step Program and reaching the twelfth step.

But, I am not in a Twelve-Step Program.

I am processing grief. The grief of my son's death.

What is the message to carry to others?

Your heart has been pierced in an indescribable way as the result of your child dying. And, grief is an emotional reaction to change. It is normal, and grief changes over time. This is how you feel now. This is how you feel today. You could not imagine you would ache in all the ways you do. Disbelief. Hopeless. Inconsolable. Weary. Angry. Depressed. Irritated. Guilty. Lonely. Scared. Nauseated. Numb. Confused. Temporary amnesia. And more.

You won't always feel this way. But today you do, and that's okay. Grief is a passage, not a place to stay. Grief is not a sign of weakness nor a lack of faith. Queen Elizabeth II said, "Grief is the price we pay for love." As someone once said, "Life is hard. Grief is hard. But taking a breath is doable." You can do that. You can take the next breath. I will help you. I will help you breathe. Breathe in through your nose for a count of four. Hold it for a count of four. Breathe out through your mouth. Hold it for a count of four. Just one breath. Okay. Now the next breath. There, you just took two breaths. Now you can take a third. Let me breathe with you.

The right way to grieve is your way. No one else is you. No one had the relationship with your child like you did. Perhaps you carried your child under your heart for nine months and the day of his birth was like no other. Elation! Or, perhaps her heart stopped beating prematurely. As moms, we carry our children in our hearts forever. And now your child has died and isn't coming home again. Those of us who believe in the afterlife of Heaven, as a result of believing in Jesus, know we will see our child again. But that doesn't help right now. Because right now is all we know. And right now, hurts.

You are allowed to feel whatever you want. Respect your feelings. Give yourself permission to feel. It can be overwhelming because you may have never felt these intense feelings before. There are no rules. No guidebook. No checklist. No schedule. No ribbon when you cross the finish line. Your feelings are neither good nor bad. They just are. And they are yours. Psychologist Gary Oliver (John Brown University), has said, "Every time you bury an emotion, you bury it alive." Mental health professionals call that "stuffing our emotions." The more you can express your feelings to a caring person who will listen to you, the better off you will feel. Eventually. You may want to seek out a professionally trained grief counselor to guide you through your grief process.

Naming your feeling is helpful. Swiss-born American psychiatrist Elisabeth Kubler-Ross (1926–2004) introduced her five-stage grief model, based on her work with terminally ill patients. This is referred to as DABDA. Denial. Anger. Bargaining. Depression. Acceptance. This is not a checklist where you receive a passing grade when accomplishing all five. Processing your grief does not necessarily fall in this order. Often it is all mixed up. However, you may find yourself feeling one or all of these emotions at some time. This is to give your feelings a name. To remind you that you are not crazy.

Denial. You may ask, "How can this be?" Or "I just talked to him this morning." Or "She was breathing in her bed last I checked." Or "You must have the wrong information." You are in a state of shock because life as you once knew it has changed in a moment of time. And you want "as you knew it" back. Denial helps you manage the initial shock.

Anger. Anger can be directed toward anyone, including your god. Professionals agree this is a necessary part of grieving and encourage it. It is important to feel the anger. Anger looks different for each person. Perhaps looking at a picture of your child and telling her how angry you are she died, is helpful. The more you feel the anger and its intensity, the more quickly you will heal and the anger will dissipate. Suppressing your anger is not healthy for either your mental or physical health.

Bargaining. This is where feeling guilty comes into grieving. "What if I had done such and such." Or "I should have." Or "If only I had seen it coming." Bargaining is a normal feeling. However, guilt and blame benefit no one. Not you, nor the people around you. Nor your child who died. You don't want to stay here, because you can't change what has happened. It is what it is.

Depression. This is a very real experience and quite normal after the death of a loved one. It is a melancholy persistent feeling of sadness resulting in a change in interest, appetite, activities, sleep pattern, and ability to function at either home, work, or both. Depression is treatable. You may want to have a health professional conduct a diagnostic evaluation and he may prescribe medication to help you produce some improvement. Talk therapy (counseling) has proven to be effective. While you probably don't feel like it, getting sleep (you may need the help of a sleep aid prescribed by a health professional), eating healthy (however, comfort food now and then can help in your recovery, as well), and just walking, will help you feel better. It is encouraged to avoid alcohol, as this is a depressant.

Know that the first year of your child's death is hard. It is the first time you will experience holidays and special events without him. You may consider a grief support group to help you learn from one another.

Acceptance. Acceptance does not ignore the loss of your child. It merely means you cannot change what has happened. Your child's death is beyond your control. It is a fact of life. It is hard to let go. It is hard to say goodbye. However, at some point, you must give yourself permission to grow as a result of your loss.

Grow. How do you grow as a result of your loss?

When you can, journal what you are feeling. Perhaps only a word is all you can write down. That is growth. Instead of focusing on what you don't have, focus on what is left. Write down one or two things each day, if you can, that you did. Example: "I got up. I ate. I sat in the chair." It is hard. But it is helping you grow through your loss.

Sometimes drawing, doing a craft, music, recreational sports, etc. will help you manage your feelings. Initially, you don't feel like doing anything that you used to enjoy. Enjoying life and your former activities will slowly come back. If you volunteered for groups you respected, getting back to volunteering will help you feel better. Maybe you want to experience things you've never tried before but always wanted to. Give yourself permission to enjoy life and laugh again.

People who have suffered loss, express compassion toward others who are grieving. Donating to a cause that is important to you, either financially or volunteering your time, helps keep your child's spirit alive. Perhaps creating a living memorial (planting a tree, etc.) in your child's name to honor her will help you feel better.

You know how terrible you initially felt at your loss. Simply showing up for a friend is all that is needed. No words of wisdom. No religious quotes. Nothing needs to be said. She won't remember what you said, anyway. But she will remember you came and sat with her. Investing in others' losses actually helps you feel better. "I see you are suffering." "I care about you." "Let's just take one breath together. I can help you breathe." "Breathe in through your nose. Count to four, and hold it for four counts. Now. Breathe out through your mouth. Count to four, and hold it for four counts. "Ok. Let's take a second one together."

And may you encourage those you are comfortable with, "How are you doing, today?" And just listen. ✂

May 7, 2020

Lament

"When my spirit was overwhelmed within me, You knew my path." (Psalm 142:3)

I don't think so. I know so. I know I don't want this pain. I've never felt this way before. Pain so indescribable and intense that it takes every ounce of energy to breathe. To focus. To even take the next step. Stomach ache all day every day. Nauseated and vomiting at bedtime. Uncontrollable bowels. Words come out in stutters as if I have a speech impediment. Just sitting and sitting and looking, because there is no energy to even get out of the chair. A glass of red wine to numb the pain. To escape the intensity.

Planning a memorial service for my son. How do you do this? How in the world do you do this? More intense pain. No family member volunteered to write my son's obituary. I asked. It was left to Mom. She carried her son under her heart for nine months and knew him longer than anyone else in the world. Mom wrote her son's obituary. Oh, the pain. The pain. Yet, the privilege of honoring my son.

The viewing. Only ten at a time could go in and show their respects, because of a stupid virus. A stupid virus that bound up normal human beings in their homes as if we were caged animals, for what was about three months. We arranged for forty friends and family to pay their respects to my son. Picking friends and family that could go in on the hour as approved by the funeral home. How can this even be? Picking friends?

You looked peaceful in the casket. I bent down and kissed the scar on your forehead. The scar where you fell off a cement yard deer and we had to rush you to the emergency room. I stroked and stroked your beard. You grew a full one. I held your hands. They were cold. No life anymore. Those were the hands I held the day you were born. So tiny and warm, and now so strong and muscular. And cold. Oh, God. Help me.

The burial of my son. Placing my boy in the ground at Cheney Country Cemetery. The pain. It just keeps flooding my entire soul. My heart just can't contain the pain. And then the next day the memorial service to honor the life of a beloved young man. Dennis paid his respects in a beautiful eulogy to our son. My heart will break in half. In half. How much can a mother take?

No energy to rise out of bed in the morning because sleep came in pockets of minutes and I'm exhausted. Time doesn't seem to exist. Just day and night. I look out the window and the sun is coming up. Again. It does that every day. But I have to get up because that is what I do every day. But I don't feel like it. I force myself to get out of bed and make it, so I won't fall back in. Just survive until the next day. Surviving until the next day is too big. Too hard. Too impossible. Okay. Just survive until you take the next breath. People put food in my mouth like I were an invalid and paralyzed because I couldn't eat. "Mom, open your mouth." "I don't feel like eating." "Mom, open your mouth and I will fill your spoon with soup and put it in your mouth." I forgot how to chew the food. "Will you show me how to chew my food? Will you breathe with me, because I forgot how to do that, as well?"

Uncontrollable shaking. I've never seen my body react like this. My hands moved in intense sporadic movement as if I were having an epileptic seizure. A seizure that I can't control and has seized my body. Holding my hands still is impossible. When I lie down in bed my legs move and thrash with such intensity that perhaps the whole bed will be shaking off its frame. The wailing. It doesn't stop.

Grief. Intense grief. The pressure is so strong on my chest. I didn't ask for this insane pain. It came the moment I learned my son died. How can my heart even keep beating? There is so much pain. Can I die of a broken heart? Yes. Maybe I will. Can I? Then I wouldn't hurt. Did Mary hurt like this when she watched her Son die? But he came back to life on the third day and she got to see Him again. My son's body stayed dead and cold in the grave. But I believe his soul is with Jesus. That is my hope. Did you meet your five siblings that

Lament | 13

went before you? Did you see your grandpas and grandmas? What was it like to see Jesus? What was it like?

Another restless, sleepless night as tears soak my pillow. I hear wailing coming through the walls and out of the rooms throughout the house as the siblings grieve the loss of their brother. As promised, the sun came up. Another day.

Anger. Anger and yelling at my son. Telling him off. How could you? Why did you? Your wife and children have been abandoned when they needed you most. You checked out of life because life got hard. It doesn't work that way, Son. You're a Midwestern, the son of two farm kids. We don't quit when the rains don't come and the crops burn up. We don't quit when the tornadoes flatten the farmstead. We don't quit when the winter blizzards kill the cattle. We don't quit when the floods prevent planting in the spring. We don't quit when it gets hard. We keep getting up in the morning. Because that's what we do. But, oh no. You quit. It got too hard. Too hard so you took the easy way out. I kick the walls until Dennis says, "Honey, stop or you're going to kick IN the walls."

Friends, family, food, condolences, cards, passersby extending a, "I don't know what to say. I don't have words." Hugs. Tears. "I'm sorry for your loss." Love in the walls. Sealed up.

Another day. Another night. A week. Then two. Then three. Then twelve weeks. Within those weeks, I heard the Holy Spirit say my name twice in my left ear. I guess I had amnesia for about a day, as I have no memory of that day. During the month of May, I saw Jordan twice for a split second. I saw him on the island in our pond in the back yard where he used to fish with his sons, and at the kitchen counter in the lower level of our house where he used to sit and work on his computer. I've seen two turtledoves sitting on my front porch, a Monarch butterfly appeared in a picture, out of nowhere, and I saw a cardinal sitting in the tree right off my deck. How does all that come together if my God is not comforting me? My intense pain is somewhat diminished. Somewhat. The hole in my heart has slightly, oh so slightly, closed, but a friend told me it never completely closes. It is always there. Always open. You just live with it.

God, your Bible teaches me in Psalm 56:8 that, "You gather up all my tears and put them in a bottle." You know my anguish and it does not go unnoticed. In Psalm 34:18 and 147:3, You comfort me with, "You are near to the brokenhearted and save those who are crushed in spirit." You tell me "You heal the brokenhearted and bind up my wounds." You also tell me in Psalm 121:4, "You never sleep." How do You do that? How does that happen? How do You take an emotionally broken vessel and bind up wounds? Too big for me to understand. Your ways are too high and too marvelous for me to grasp.

I just trust the best way I know how. Sometimes a little. Sometimes a lot. I hope I can keep serving others even though I carry my own sorrow wherever I go. That is all I can do. Psalm 40:3 comforts me, "He put a new song in my mouth, a song of praise to our God; Many will see and fear and will trust in the Lord."

Granting forgiveness and mercy to my son. Because God is God. And I am not. ✀

June 9, 2020

Learning to Live Without my Son

My grandson told me twice that his dad and Jesus were both thirty-three when they died. I think a little boy who misses his dad finds comfort there was something special about both of them dying at the same age. Perhaps. And yet, neither one's death makes sense to me. How can it be that someone would die for my sins? Someone I have never met, but trusted forty-two years ago, and felt His Holy Spirit fill my soul from the top of my head to the bottom of my feet. I was changed in a moment of time. I have stayed changed. I know Jesus saved me because I walk by faith and not by sight.

And the other one, my son, whom we prayed for before he was conceived in my womb. I carried him nine months and delivered him into the world in a rush with only four contractions, still in his intact amniotic sac, an en caul or veiled birth, at his entrance. This rare delivery happens one in eighty thousand births. Both are unique individuals. Both contribute to society. Both made an impact on my life.

Learning to live without my son is the hardest thing I have ever had to do. I don't see how my heart can break anymore.

I don't know how the gaping hole can ever mend. I'm told it doesn't. It might close up somewhat, but it never goes away. A friend told me he has lived with the hole in his heart for over twenty years since his daughter died. I'm tired of hurting. I'm tired of crying. I'm tired of forcing a smile because I know I need to. I'm tired of trying to live without my son. But I know I need to. I have to. I have to somehow find meaning in his unexpected death. If I didn't love my son so much, I wouldn't hurt so much. I didn't stop loving him when he died. Death cannot destroy my love for him.

Finding meaning. How does that work? Finding meaning in my son's death? I think that means living in a way that honors him but doesn't put him on a pedestal. I suppose this will come as time marches on. I like to think now, though, I am building on the foundational blocks he established with his wife and family. He built into his children the love of the outdoors. He taught them to love Jesus and took them to Sunday School and church. He taught them to pray. He respected both of us as his parents, as well as his parents-in-law. I have the opportunity to invest in those young lives several times a week. Not to replace him as their father, but to encourage them to continue with what their dad loved and taught them.

I guess that is where I can start to find meaning in the death of my son. To love the things and people he loved. And to carry those things into the next generation.

Two lives.

One to cover my sins.

One to continue his legacy.

August 17, 2020

Sunday Will Never Be the Same

I don't know if the pain from learning of my son's death is greater, or the ache from realizing what never will be. There is a hole in my heart that never closes. It's always decreasing or increasing in size, but never goes away. And I have to live with it for the rest of my life. I would say, "I must then be partially disabled." Partially disabled because a part of me can never be fixed. I don't know if I will ever be able to mentally perform at full capacity again. Maybe. But it doesn't feel like it today. I am not talking about the heart in a literal sense, but in the feeling part buried somewhere deep inside. Deep inside where human hands of the heart surgeon cannot even get to. Deep inside where God lives and filled me with His Holy Spirit.

In my counseling room, I would often tell my clients, "I work with the part you can't see, but the part you can feel." You can feel an emotion, happy, sad, depressed, joy, fear, anger; but, how do you touch it or see it? The expression on the outside is a result of an emotion we experience in the mind and feel in our hearts. We can observe if someone is happy by the expression on their face; sad by the tears running down their cheeks; and depressed by the way they sit, stand,

and walk. We can observe someone who is fearful by the way their limbs tremble or their voice quivers. Someone who is angry may have clenched fists and/or a tight jaw. And there are more emotions. As a licensed mental health professional, I would observe my client's behavior in the counseling room by what she was not saying.

It has been nearly six months since my son's death. I have been told people grieve at their own pace and in their own way. In fact, I often told my clients those same words when I was walking them through grief. So, I really don't know what my own pace is. I'm breathing, eating, hydrating, and sleeping. The cards and notes of sympathy still arrive in the mail. I am overwhelmed by people's love and support for us. And I read each line of the card and each handwritten message with the love the sender must have put into each word. E-mails and texts still come in with the sender saying, "Just thinking of you." I have people that check on me daily as well as weekly, and they may ask, "How are you doing today?" I learned how to answer that question with, "I'm learning to live without my son."

I can get through a day without crying. Yet, the next day the tsunami of grief may invade my soul and I am knocked off my feet. I can produce a heartfelt smile. I can drive and remember where I am going, and I can find my way back home without getting lost. I can read something for fun and relaxation, besides suicide loss survivors' stories and counseling books and articles, and not feel guilty for reading for pleasure. My short-term memory is not back where I am comfortable, but I do find I have pockets of satisfaction when I can remember what I had for supper the night before!

My life has been divided into two parts: "Before my son died, and after my son died." The American sunshine rock band (Spanky and our Gang) recorded and released (1967), "Sunday Will Never Be the Same." The singer has broken up with her man, the love affair is over, and all she has left is memories of spending Sundays together. The call came to me from my husband telling me of Jordan's death at 1:49 pm Sunday, March 15, 2020. Sunday will never be the same.

September 2, 2020

I've Got This

Twice I have seen and heard Jesus talk to me—once in a vision and once in a dream. I don't think I've ever put much faith in dreams because I sometimes wake up with nightmares, sweating, screaming, shaking, crying, and Dennis having to bring me out of the dream and calm me down. Sometimes I cannot remember what happened, or if I do, it is short-lived and it really doesn't bother me in the morning. However, at two specific times, I can remember my conversation with Jesus.

The first time I saw Jesus was when I was delivering my sixth baby, June 2, 1993. During the intense pain and labor, I asked for an epidural. According to my labor nurse, I had waited too long for pain relief and she told me it was too late and to deliver without an epidural, as I had with the five previous babies. I didn't believe her and asked her to send for a doctor to give me one anyway. He arrived shortly, and after an examination told me it was too late, as I'd be delivering in a few minutes. I said, "What do I do now?" The physician said, "I'm sorry, you're on your own."

I immediately had a vision that I was standing at Heaven's gate. Jesus was on my left and several people were standing in front of him. I could not see their faces or identify who they might be. The people standing said, "What do we do now?" (Meaning they wanted to get into Heaven and could not). I specifically saw and heard Jesus say, "I'm sorry, you're on your own." That vision has stayed with me since that day. The words of Jesus I can still hear in my head. I understood him to mean, "You can't get into Heaven after you die. It's too late. You had a lifetime to make a decision, and you didn't." I knew Heaven was secure as my eternity.

The second time I saw Jesus was in a dream I had on September 7, 2020. In my dream, I saw Jesus (the same face, clothes, and voice as I saw and heard in 1993). He was walking toward me, and I saw someone dodge behind him. I only saw his back. I know for sure it was Jordan behind him. Jesus said, "I've got this." I was comforted that my son is being taken care of.

I think of a vision as something I see in my mind, but I'm not sleeping and I can remember it. A dream is something I am aware of at some level during sleep. God spoke to Joseph in the Bible in a dream about seven years of plenty followed by seven years of famine. Daniel had dreams about beasts. The Magi were directed in a dream not to go back to Herod. Joseph, Jesus's early father, had two dreams: (1) To not divorce Mary, and (2) a dream to get up immediately, (he, Mary, and the Baby Jesus), and go to Egypt. The apostle

John was exiled to Patmos Island and had a dream about a beast coming out of the sea. And, there were more.

So, I guess, God can still speak to people today, and I believe He did. He brought me comfort both times.

September 13, 2020

Riding the Waves

As I live with the intense grief over the death of our son and Conklin Director, I have several thoughts I am going to write down. They are in no particular order, they just are.

Grief has no timetable. Grief is a natural response to loss. My grief for my son started the moment Dennis called and told me he had died. Our son's earthly life was now past tense. His life as I once knew it was no more. Love and grief come together. I loved Jordan deeply; therefore, I grieve deeply. Grief comes in waves. It will have its own way. I try to ride waves. I try to be patient with myself and let my grief naturally unfold. At times, I get frustrated with myself because I can't control my tears, and they come at the most inconvenient times. I let them flow. I am broken and putting pieces back together. Life has its peaks and valleys. I'm present in both.

We each had a relationship with Jordan in our own way. No one else is you. No one else is me. No one else had the relationship with my son as I did, mother and son. My lifeblood. A privilege. I am still Jordan's mother. As a mom, I will carry Jordan, as well as my other children, in my heart forever. That cannot change.

I am giving myself permission to feel my emotions. I can't heal what I can't feel. My emotions are overwhelming because I've never grieved this intensely before. The feelings move through me. Naming my feelings has been helpful: sad, frustrated, angry, okay, not okay, denial, tired, love, and more. I don't ignore my pain or keep it inside. In order for me to heal, I am facing my grief and dealing with it the best I know how.

I have written several journal entries. Writing helps me process what is inside my heart. Life gives us many avenues to traverse, and I am trying to make the most of this journey. A journey I will travel the rest of my life. Both Dennis and I have invested multiple hours of counseling with a licensed grief and trauma counselor who guides us through our grief, encouraging us many times to just keep breathing. Just. Keep. Breathing. Because sometimes breathing is all I can do.

One day at a time is too hard. One step at a time is too far. But, one breath, one tear at a time, is doable.

People who have suffered loss, express compassion toward others who are grieving. Many times people have said to me, "If there is anything I can do for you, let me know." To that I want to respond, "There is no greater gift you can give someone who is grieving than to ask them about their loved one, and how they are doing today. Then truly listen." Ignoring a person's loss is devastating. I have had friends call and ask, "How are you doing." I respond with, "I'm learning to live without my son." I am honest with them. I share how I am feeling the day they contacted me.

To those of you folks who have grieved with Dennis and me, I am more grateful than I even have words to express. The condolences still keep coming and coming and coming. I hope I can be as good a friend to all of you as you have been to me.

I am gradually finding meaning in Jordan's death. There is pain in the loss, but there is also good. I don't want to stay with this pain, but I will ride the waves. I want to help find meaning in Jordan's death. I don't know what that looks like. I'm not there. I do have joy, though, when I see my children and grandchildren keep moving on. I have joy when I see the siblings encouraging each other in their loss. I have joy when I see how family, friends, neighbors, work associates, and church folks have surrounded a young widow and her four young children, and support her with love, comfort, food, carpooling, child care, and gifts. They just keep serving and serving and serving.

And I have joy when so many of you have told me how Jordan impacted your life. That will be his legacy.

October 21, 2020

Two Pillars

Two pillars majestically stand just inside the front door of my house. To the guests walking into my house through the front door, they pass by them on the left as they walk past the dining room into the living room, kitchen, and sunroom. While they look impressive in anyone's opinion, they were actually placed there by the builder to hold up my house! If I were to remove one or both of them, well, I don't know. I suppose the whole second story would collapse in my living room. Not a good idea. They have been the discussion of many a guest and family member. When we serve guests in the dining room and we set up the table and chairs, someone always has to maneuver their chair around the pillars. We have taken numerous pictures of people posing around the pillars. Grandchildren have literally climbed them as if they were outside scaling a tree.

Yet, as I reflect on these two pillars, I internalize what these two pillars mean to me. Not just a structural necessity to hold up my house; rather, how tangible objects become intangible to me as I learn how to encourage those folks around me.

Our Bible teaches us King Solomon built a Temple to honor God, (1 Kings 7:15–22, 41–42). He commissioned

Two Pillars | **29**

a renowned artisan from the tribe of Naphtali to create two massive columns that stood on either side of the front door. They were made of cast bronze, with the top of the pillars elaborately decorated with bowl-shaped bronze lilies, 200 pomegranates in two rows, and seven "nets of network and twisted threads of chain work." They stood 34.5 feet tall and measured 18 feet around the middle. They were freestanding structures. They didn't hold up anything. They were just there. King Solomon gave them names: The one on the left as you entered the Temple, was named Boaz, meaning "Strong in Him." The one on the right he named Jachin, meaning "He will establish." Solomon was granted wisdom from God as not seen on the earth before or after (1 Kings 3:12). We can assume, therefore, his naming of these pillars was impressed upon him by God, perhaps Boaz was named for King David (Solomon's father), and Jachin was named for himself, Solomon. Perhaps. A pillar can stand alone (as in Solomon's Temple) or it can be a stabilizing function (as in my house). A pillar can add beauty to a structure.

Well, I didn't name my pillars. Never even thought about it. Rather, what I think of is being stable in my mind and well-being to give strength, comfort, and support to others. Let me explain how I do that:

Strength: To me, this means managing challenges, frustrations, and setbacks as they come into my life. My foundation for what is right and wrong is my Bible. It teaches me ethics to live by. We oftentimes confuse the words ethics and morals. Actually, the two words have different meanings.

Ethics comes from the Greek word ethos, meaning a "stall" for horses, a place of stability and permanence. Ethics is absolute and a set of standards. The word 'morals' describes the shifting behavioral pattern of society. When the behavior of society and the culture makes the norms, we have shifting sand and nothing is absolute. It is like a river, always changing. A few decades ago that which was unthinkable, gradually became acceptable.

Comfort: It means offering a guest to our home a chair and a cup of cool water. It means intentionally listening, and not interrupting when a friend is distraught. It means trying not to fix his/her life. It means asking questions and not judging. It means, perhaps, easing a person's feelings of grief or distress and caring for a despairing person.

Support: To me, this means taking care of my emotional and physical needs to be healthy enough to hold up and add strength to a person's life. To carry the weight of someone else who is emotionally broken. To be their brace so they don't collapse emotionally or physically. To validate their feelings. To not give up on him/her.

My desire is to stay grounded in my ethos so that I can be a comfort and support to those whose worlds are falling apart. ✿

November 18, 2020

Coming Back

I never thought I'd be here. Right where I am today. In the middle of a broken heart trying to climb my way out. I could not have imagined I'd be trying to survive from a place of intense brokenness. I could not have imagined, when we married over forty-seven years ago, what my future would hold. I could not have imagined I'd belong to The Club Nobody Wants to Belong to. I thought we'd live happily ever after. Oh, that's right, that's only in fairy tales. Whatever that means. My future didn't include nine years of infertility challenges, surgeries, and the loss of five preterm babies. It didn't include watching my dreams and aspirations disintegrate in front of my eyes and not being able to do anything about it.

It didn't include starting a business and living solely on commission and being scared we'd not have enough to cover expenses. It didn't include friends and loved ones divorcing. It didn't include friends and loved ones challenged with addictions and depression. It didn't include losing an adult child to suicide. It didn't include both Dennis and me living with and managing our depression. I didn't know I could cry so many tears over friends and loved ones, both rejoicing and heartbroken.

One. Tear. At. A. Time.

But, God knew. He knew I couldn't have imagined. So that's why He has taken care of me for more years than I even know. I recently read the testimony of someone who was managing the loss of a family member. He said, "Each tear has a story to be told." I reflect on the words of King David in Psalm 56:8 when he writes, "God collects all my tears and puts them in a bottle." He is keeping track of my human sorrow. How does that work? What does He do with my tears in my bottle? What does He do with my human suffering and broken heart? I want to believe He never forgets my sadness. My tears. My weariness. My crying out for relief from the heavy burden of emotional pain. I want to believe He customizes a recovery plan, just for me, because I am made in His image and my fingerprints are unique to me. Unique.

I'm coming back, though. Rebuilding. There are days the fog of grief has lifted. Then it's back again. It takes a long time to pick up the pieces. Changes don't happen all at once, either. And that's okay. I'm actually doing something I thought was impossible. For nearly a year now, I'm learning to live without my son. I have landed in a place I never knew existed. Somehow in my mind, I believed when we crossed the midnight threshold of 2021, I'd look at my losses differently. Yet, when I woke up on the first day of 2021, I felt as if a shroud of darkness was covering my body and I couldn't get out. I cried. You see, the calendar didn't know it was supposed to leave my grief in 2020. It just came with me.

Coming Back | **33**

I encountered a number of significant losses within a one-year period. They were, and are, a part of my life. I grieved them. I'm doing what I can to come back. A friend asked me during lunch late last summer, "Do you believe God is good all the time?" I hesitated. I said, "Not right now." Today, January 13, 2021, as I write this journal entry, My heart can say, "God is good all the time." I trust Him the best I can, even when it looks bleak to me. And yet, as many losses as I believe I have grieved this past year, I have been blessed.

I am grateful for Dennis and each one of my family members. I am grateful I was present during the birth of one of my grandchildren. I am grateful each of my children at a young age learned about Jesus. I am grateful my children love each other. I am grateful for the day Dennis proposed marriage to me (Dec. 25, 1972), and the day we married (Aug. 24, 1973). I'm grateful I trusted Jesus as my Lord and Savior (June 25, 1978).

I am grateful, so grateful, for the many individuals, family members, friends, and neighbors who have invested in my life.

And, I felt I started coming back when, about six months after my son's death, I asked my nail technician to polish my nails black, a color I only dare to put on if I'm feeling pretty good, and pretty confident about myself! I'm coming back.

January 14, 2021

On the Eve of the First Anniversary of my Son's Death

It poured rain last night and most of today. Pretty typical for a Nebraska spring. One day we have snow. The next day spring rains. The next day the sun shines all day. Then it starts all over again for a few weeks. Birds sing and wake us before dawn as signs of life pop up all over after a cold and long winter. The grass is greening up, buds coming on the trees, flowers breaking through the dirt saying, "Remember me? I slept underground all winter and I'm back. It's okay to pick me and bring me inside to brighten up your table." We hear the laughter of children as they can once again run outside without shoes and splash and jump in puddles of water.

Someone told me that Nebraskans are the toughest in the country. Resilient. That's a big responsibility. Perhaps, it comes quite naturally living in the Great American Desert. Perhaps, we have no choice. Maybe it is all we know. Pioneers passed through our treeless, semi-arid grassland, and what seemed unfit for farming region, as quickly as possible en route to what they considered to be better land and better living in the west. A few decided to stay and homestead. My roots. Dennis's roots. Our children's roots. Our roots go deep.

On the Eve of the First Anniversary of my Son's Death | **35**

Psychologists define resilience as, "The process of adapting well in the face of adversity, trauma, and tragedy." Why is it, then, that some folks have resilience and some do not? Resilience is available to each of us at any time and anywhere.

The bottom line is, stuff happens. We are not guaranteed a stress-free or sorrow-free life. No one is immune. No one is discriminated against. And by all means, it is not that we welcome it in, either! It is what we do with the tough times that creates resilience. We can either accept the fact that stuff happens, or we can have a "woe is me" attitude and blame everyone. We can think and act in ways to learn resilience and to move through tough times.

Resilient folks carefully choose where to focus their attention. In Twelve-step programs, meetings often start with the Serenity Prayer, "God, grant me the serenity to accept the things I cannot change; courage to change the things I can; and wisdom to know the difference." Learning to let go with what I cannot change, or what is not my business, allows me the mental freedom to focus on what I can change; that being how I react to situations. It is easy to be negative. It seems our world thrives on the worst-case scenarios and pumps it into our social media for us to ingest and then digest. I choose, rather, to find things to be grateful for and focus my attention on. "Whatever is true, whatever is honorable, whatever is pure, whatever is lovely, whatever is of good repute, and if there is any excellence and if anything worthy of praise, dwell on these things" (Phil. 4:8). I believe resilient people ask themselves, "Is what I'm doing helping or harming me to stay positive?" I try to be aware of my thoughts as well as my behavior patterns. Writing down each day a couple of things I am grateful for helps me focus on what I have left. I really have a lot left. I really have much to be grateful for.

And so it goes.

March 14, 2021

Recovery — The Twelfth Step

The waves of grief still come. Oh, not as often and not so intense, but they come. They come unexpectedly when life seems to be going along just fine. There will never be a last tear for my son as the tears fill my eyes and roll down my cheeks and drop on my shirt. Usually, I'm alone. Alone in my sadness, missing my boy. I ride the waves because I can't get out from under them. I'm drowning as they overwhelm me, but I eventually come up for air and I go on. Go on to what? With whom? How? Life is different now that I permanently carry this hole in my heart.

Does anyone see the hole I carry inside me? Can they see through my soul to the emptiness where Jordan lived? Did the lady standing behind me in the grocery story know my son died a little over a year ago? No, how would she? Does the wait staff taking my order want me to tell him I'm still sad over my son's death? Maybe. But then he has to get to the next table. And the sales associate who sells me a pair of shoes, does she know my son died? She wouldn't know, either. And when the makeup artist at the counter asked me, "How have you been? I haven't seen you for a while. Let me show you our new line." Does he really want to know? Maybe he does. Maybe he doesn't. I silently ask myself if they care, but maybe they do care. Maybe they have experienced unimaginable grief and are faking it through the day. Maybe they need someone to just listen to them. But, we all know, life is full of people faking it, just to get through the day. I don't want to be one of them.

I don't apologize when the grief waves come. There is nothing to apologize for. It is what it is, and it will have its way. I have asked each one of my children several times how they are doing after their brother's death. "Doing okay, Mom." I believe they are doing what they can to keep moving through life. Some of my children cry on the phone when I talk to them. Some don't. I respect that. Some of them do most of the talking, and I just get to listen. And with some of them, I do most of the talking. That is all okay. We don't talk about Jordan so much anymore. I mean, we do, but not with every conversation. I have asked his wife several times how she is doing. Her responses have been honest and sometimes flooded with tears. And we hug. And that's okay, as well.

A broken heart knows no borders. It crosses cultures, ethnicities, ages, genders, generations, and religions. It enters the hearts of the rich and the famous, as well as the homeless. It affects pets and their owners. There is no way around it, a broken heart takes time, and hard work, to heal. I'm in recovery from my son's unexpected death. I've come a long way from where I was a year ago. Both my physical and mental health are healing. And that's where the twelfth step comes in, as in a recovery program, "Having had a spiritual awakening as the result of these steps (Steps: One to Eleven), we tried to carry this message to others and to practice these principles in all our affairs." By investing in those who are hurting, I continue to heal.

April 23, 2021

A Semicolon and a Green Ribbon

The month of May is designated as Mental Health Awareness Month. While the definition of mental health can be subjective, it merely is a health condition involving changes in our thinking, emotions, or behavior (all, or a combination of the above). Mental illness is associated with family, work, or social activities. Mental illness is treatable if we get help working through our frustrations. Common examples of mental illness are mood disorders, anxiety, psychotic disorders, dementia, and eating disorders.

I am reminded of my own mental illness over twenty-nine years ago. I didn't know what depression was at the time. I was overwhelmed with tears and a lack of energy (I was pregnant with our fifth baby at the time, which contributed to my lack of energy). As a Christian, I tried to pray myself out of my depression. I tried to justify I had nothing to be depressed about. I reviewed my Scripture memory verses to help me feel better. But I was still overwhelmed. I cried because I couldn't get out of the black hole I seemed to be falling into. There was no ladder to climb out. Finally, I sought out a licensed mental health counselor and made my first appointment. Making that first call for an appointment, then actually walking into my first session, was very hard. I had a stigma about seeking a mental health counselor. Counseling was for someone else, not me.

I didn't know what a counseling session looked like, so I took my notebook and pen and was going to take notes as if I were attending a class. However, the moment I sat down in my counselor's office, I couldn't even see my paper as the tears flooded my vision and ran down my face. I cried the entire session. I don't even remember what was said, other than my counselor asked if I wanted to come back for another session. "Yes, I guess so. And talk again? Is there more to talk about?" And, I kept going back. And going back. And going back.

I gradually got better over about eighteen months. Oh, not all at once, but I got better. In fact, I liked how I now felt and wanted to invest in other women who also may be feeling overwhelmed. I didn't think I was the only one out there. I took classes and became a lay counselor with my church and started ministering with empathy to the brokenhearted. It was a privilege to be invited into the brokenness of another person's heart and walk with them through their frustrations and challenges. I later earned my Bachelor of Science Degree in Biblical Studies and my Master of Arts Degree in both Biblical Studies and Psychology. I studied and passed the National Mental Health Counselor's Exam, and opened up my mental health counseling practice. I like to think I have a listening and teaching ministry.

I have been invited to present seminars on Christian Pastoral Counseling for hundreds of indigenous pastors and church leaders in both Mexico and India. I have written a program entitled Paraclete, which has been translated into seven languages. Paraclete is the Greek term for Holy Spirit who "comes alongside as a Counselor or Advocate." I stay mentally healthy by investing in others when I come alongside another brokenhearted soul, and when I encourage others to do the same through listening skills that I teach in these seminars.

While studying the Christian Bible, memorizing Bible verses, and praying, are all certainly important in helping us climb out of a black hole of depression, sometimes we also need the help of a trained and professional mental health counselor to guide us to recovery. It's okay to ask for help. Asking for help is not a sign of weakness, but rather a sign of strength. Because if we don't get help, I believe we just keep falling and falling deeper into the black hole.

Please, my dear reader, don't go there. It's perfectly alright to ask for help when life hands you challenges. It's okay. Please get help.

So why a semicolon and a green ribbon? Because your story isn't over. An author uses a semicolon in their writing projects because they choose to continue their sentence, separating two independent clauses that relate to each other. The semicolon encourages us to continue with life because

A Semicolon and a Green Ribbon | **43**

YOU are the author of your story. And as long as you are breathing, you have much to offer. The green ribbon reminds us that May is Mental Health Awareness Month.

How do we take care of ourselves? Here are some suggestions:

Talk to a trusted friend or professional therapist about your feelings.

Keep active. Make time for your hobbies and favorite projects. I enjoy color art therapy.

Eat your greens. Drink your greens.

Drink eight glasses of water/day.

Maintain a reasonable weight.

Avoid smoking and vaping. Keep alcohol to a minimum.

Exercise—whatever is appropriate for your physical health.

Get enough sleep. Sleep behaviorists want us to get 7–8 hours a night. Sleep allows our body and mind to recharge.

Surround yourself with positive and encouraging people.

Do something every day that is a routine for you.

Set some kind of positive goal each day. Invest in other people. Learn to listen and not interrupt.

A few minutes every day sitting in front of the window enjoying the sun, even if it's cloudy, is healthy and healing.

The above are suggestions I try to practice each day. Some days I do better than others; but regardless, I do something each day.

Doing something is better than doing nothing.

May 7, 2021

Stewarding my Pain

I was raised in the Midwest on a farm with no running water or indoor plumbing. I have risen above my childhood roots, and have traveled to over thirty countries. While my Midwestern roots may seem to some like a sheltered life, it actually is quite the opposite. I learned to live off the land and endure when life on the farm got hard. It did not make me weak. It made me strong. I am the first generation in my family to receive a college degree. In my worldly travels, I have seen the very rich. I have seen the very poor. I have seen the living. I have seen the dead.

In order to gauge the character of a city, I believe you need to interact with its people. I have ministered in Mexico multiple times. I sat on tires in the dirt and through an interpreter, counseled the distraught. I have served with a medical team and helped children learn to brush their teeth. I have held Bible studies in a women's prison in Mexico, as well as taught in a men's rehab center. I have started a women's support group and Bible study in the park in Ensenada. I have sat in the dirt and on rocks with the homeless and hopeless, held their crusty and dirty hands, and prayed with them. I have fed the hungry. Clothed the naked. Encouraged the fainthearted.

And I cried. I took a breath. I lived. I walked on.

I have walked through the Dharavi slum in Mumbai, the world's largest slum, where 600,000 souls live in an area half the size of Central Park in New York. I was impressed. The people were happy. Everyone from the youngest to the oldest was working. No one was waiting around for a handout. It was a city within a city. Children played and laughed in the most unsanitary conditions I have ever seen. I have seen entire families living on garbage dumps, along with rotten food and human and animal feces. I have seen the dying in the streets in India when there was nothing I could do to help them and we had to pass them by. I have held dying babies at Mother Teresa's home for the Orphans and Abandoned Children in Kolkata. And I have taken off my shoes at the tomb of Saint (Mother) Teresa and on bent knee prayed and thanked God for her ministry.

And I cried. I took a breath. I lived. I walked on.

I stood at the bedside of my dad and held his hand as he took his last breath. It was a holy moment to usher him into the Kingdom. I sat with my sister-in-law as she lay dying in her hospital bed.

And I cried. I took a breath. I lived. I walked on.

Was I ready when my husband called me at 1:49 pm on March 15, 2020, and through his tears, told me "He's gone."?

No. Was I ready to enter into the most intense and excruciating physical and mental pain I have ever felt grieving the loss of my son? No.

And I cried. I took a breath. I lived. I walked on.

Was I ready when loved ones were challenged with depression and addictions? No.

And I cried. I took a breath. I lived. I walked on.

Was I ready for Covid-19 to enter our lives and have friends and families isolated from each other for a year? No.

And I cried. I took a breath. I lived. I walked on.

Was I ready when I was sexually assaulted a number of years ago? No.

And I cried. I took a breath. I lived. I walked on.

Was I ready when my husband and I grieved the loss of five preterm babies and nine years of infertility? No.

And I cried. I took a breath. I lived. I walked on.

Frederick Buechner encourages us to "steward your pain." He teaches us to stay in touch with our pain and to be open to the pain of others. By my taking the risk to be open and reaching out to the broken places in another's heart, another level of healing takes place. I don't know or understand how it works. It just does.

And yet, I suppose the Jordan-sized hole will never close up, lest I forget to stay in touch with my pain and be a good steward.

This past year I have had the privilege to minister to several families who have lost children by suicide, as well as a friend who lost his beloved sister by electrocution. I continue to minister to the widow who lost her husband less than a year ago.

Was I ready to push through the pain of my son's death to extend a hand to those who were hurting? No. But I did it anyway because my grief counselor, who has walked with my husband and me every step of the way since our son's death, encouraged me to invest in other people. Because being a good steward of my pain, helps heal my own heart.

And I cried. I took a breath. I lived. I walked on.

May 11, 2021

Into the Storm

The brave pioneers who left Independence, Missouri, in the mid-1800s to cross the Great American Desert on their way to an anticipated better life in Oregon, had countless challenges crossing Nebraska. You can drive to western Nebraska and see the wagon ruts of the migrants who made their way across the prairie. But what you don't see are the unmarked graves of the husbands, wives, mothers, fathers, children, family members, friends, pets, and livestock who didn't make it to Oregon. Many people died along the way, and their stories lie beneath the surface of the ground. The survivors buried their loved ones on the path in shallow unmarked graves, just deep enough so wild animals wouldn't dig up their bodies. And, they kept walking, packing down the graves as each person walked on the graves and as wagon traffic flowed westward toward Oregon.

A friend encouraged me many times after the death of my son, to Just. Keep. Walking. Toward. Oregon. Just. Keep. Walking.

My son had a tattoo of an American Bison (also known as the buffalo) on his left shoulder. Before he went to the tattoo parlor, he asked me if I wanted to go and watch. Since I had never seen a tattoo being made, I said I would like to do that. I asked him how he decided on an American Bison for his second tattoo. He told me he did the research, and because Bison once roamed the Great American Plains, it reminded him of his roots, Nebraska. He told me he was very particular about how his tattoo came out, so he carefully looked at several designs before deciding. I watched as the tattoo artist created my son's tattoo in full color. After Jordan's death, several of his siblings and his wife got a tattoo of a Bison on their arm to remind them of their brother and husband.

I, too, did my research on the American Bison. While the Bison and the domestic cow belong to the same family and are quite similar in their grazing habits, it has been claimed that cattle are domestic Bison. Bison wander more than domestic cattle. Bison once roamed and ranged across North America. It is estimated there were 75 million Bison at one time. As far as the eye could see, it was believed the Plains were covered by one enormous mass of Bison. Those pioneers would have lived among the Bison as they traveled west. But due to hide and sport hunting by the late 1800s, they were near a point of extinction.

Cows in a thunderstorm are in a very vulnerable position. As a storm approaches, they turn and run away from the storm, heading in the opposite direction hoping to outrun the storm. They may seek shelter under a tree, one of the most dangerous spots during a thunder and lightning storm.

They receive the brunt of the storm. However, cows cannot outrun storms!

On the other hand, as Bison roam the Plains and as a storm rolls in from the west, Bison will turn and charge directly into the storm, taking it head-on. The Bison's massive hump made up of muscles and long vertebrae, uses its head as a snowplow in winter, swinging side to side sweeping aside the snow. By running towards the storm, and ultimately straight through the storm, they experience a minimum amount of pain, time, frustration, and amount of exposure to the storm.

The symbolism of the Bison heading into the storm reminds me of how to confront life's challenges. We all have storms, both professionally and personally. The most difficult thing I have ever had to experience is my son's death. I could not have imagined the emotional and physical stress I would experience. It seemed I would never stop crying. I felt I would never stop hurting. I didn't avoid my grief and loss. I didn't block it out. I got help. I was like the Bison, charging directly into the storm. By ignoring and avoiding my pain and grief, it would have taken longer to recover, much like the cows who run away from the storm.

The only way through the pain and stress was into the storm. No human could take my pain from me and carry it for me. Nor could they feel the hole in my heart from my son's death. No one could cry my tears for me. I had to grieve in my way. Many empathized with my sorrow. Lifting us in prayer with love.

As I write this last chapter, it has been over fourteen months since our son died. I believe I can say I am through the worst part of the storm, and I actually feel the storm clouds lifting. I can see light and feel the sunshine. I have ridden the waves of grief more times than I can remember, and I always got through them. I didn't hide my grief or apologize. I just rode it out, and eventually, that wave passed.

"Blessed be the God and Father of our Lord Jesus Christ, the Father of all mercies and God of all comfort, who comforts us in all our affliction so that we will be able to comfort those who are in any affliction with the comfort with which we ourselves are comforted by God" (2 Cor. 1:3-4).

And I cried. I took a breath. I lived. I walked on.

May 26, 2021

If you have a grief journey you would like to share, come walk with me.

pattynun.whcc@gmail.com

www.ingramcontent.com/pod-product-compliance
Lightning Source LLC
Chambersburg PA
CBHW070107100426
42743CB00012B/2670